THE
BORN
AGAIN
PANACEA
SYNDROME

LAYING A FOUNDATION
FOR SPIRITUAL GROWTH

PASTOR LOUIS N. OTEY JR.

urbanpress.

The Born Again Panacea Syndrome
by Pastor Louis N. Otey, Jr.
Copyright © 2020 Louis N. Otey, Jr.

ISBN # 978-1-63360-141-3

For Worldwide Distribution Printed in the U.S.A.

Urban Press
P.O. Box 8881
Pittsburgh, PA 15221-0881 USA
412.646.2780
www.urbanpress.us

This book is dedicated to my loving, caring, beautiful, and committed wife, Debra Otey, who is my greatest supporter. Thank you for believing in me, and for your loving and aggressive encouragement that led to the completion of this book.

INTRODUCTION

I am motivated to write this book because I want to share with you some of the things I have learned during my twenty years of being a pastor, a substance abuse counselor for the Air National Guard, and a certified biblical counselor—as well as walking with the Lord for more than 46 years.

I also write because I am frustrated along with other committed believers as I increasingly encounter people who are looking for spiritual shortcuts. Some have been taught and believed that if they come to the Lord, all their problems will be solved or, better yet, they won't have any (or as many) problems. The Apostle Paul wrote in Romans 14:17, "The Kingdom of God is not meat and drink but righteousness peace and joy in the Holy Spirit." These words have caused me to ask the question, *If the Kingdom of God produces righteousness, peace, and joy, why is it that many professing Christians are frustrated with life, full of anger, fear, in despair, out of control, confused, and troubled in so many ways?*

We profess to serve a God who has given us 66 books of revelation that contain the answers to all our problems. Despite this, many Christians are not experiencing the benefits of what the Kingdom of God offers. What most do not understand is that the feelings of hopelessness, frustration, and fear are designed by God to cause a person to seek earnestly the kingdom of God. The kingdom of God will not prevent their problems but will give them a way to deal with their problems, which may include suffering and pain.

What is the Kingdom of God? It is the rule, dominion, and governmental control of God in a person's life. When God is ruling and in control, those things that negatively impact one's life will be replaced with the promised righteousness, peace, and joy. Jesus said it best when He taught, "Seek first the Kingdom of God and his righteousness and all of those things that you have need of shall be added unto you" (Matthew 6:33).

That word *seek* means *to crave, to look for with a sense of urgency, to be unwilling to be satisfied with anything less* than God's governmental control in one's life. It is to come to the place where one would rather die than live outside of God's governmental control. It is to passionately say to God, *I will not accept anything but Your righteousness being manifested in and through my life. I will be, I must be in right standing with you. My life will reflect your righteousness in my actions or take me now.* It is to be hungry and thirsty to comply with God's divine will in purpose, thought, and action.

Jesus also stated, "He that hungers and thirst for righteousness shall be filled" (Matthew 5:6). How hungry are you? How thirsty are you? This will determine the passion that drives you to seek the Kingdom of God. It's not about God solving your problems like some cosmic counselor or butler. It is about you discovering what it is in your life that is blocking God's promised peace and joy and then correcting it to align with God's requirements for His blessings.

Everyone deals with conscious and unconscious bondages—things like fear, worry, past hurts, rejection—but the Bible does not spend a lot of time discussing them even though we know that everyone has a struggle with them. The reason we see very little emphases on these issues of low self-esteem, anger, rage, and the like is because the gospel of the Kingdom is the medicine that treats these. While the Scripture mentions them, it does not spend a lot of time telling us how to overcome them through the use of so-called inner-healing techniques or going back into our childhood and digging up old hurts to resolve unfinished business. It simply says "put them aside" (see Colossians 3:8). If we truly believe that the Bible has all the answers for life's issues, then why do we look outside of Scripture to deal with these issues?

When dealing with these conscious and unconscious bondages, there are three necessary foundation stones that must first be laid in your life in order to deal with these issues. Those three are: repentance that leads to salvation, water baptism, and the baptism of the Holy Spirit. Let's take a brief look as to why these foundation stones are necessary.

Repent and believe the gospel. We must repent from the dead works that can't help us, and we must rely on Christ's finished work on the cross. When we repent, we die to sin and turn away from our old lifestyle. At that point, we become spiritually alive and set free from the bondages of the power of sin. We are also transferred out of the kingdom of darkness into the kingdom of light of His dear Son, experiencing being born again through the indwelling presence of the Spirit of God.

Water baptism. Every death must have a burial. When you are baptized after being saved, you are identifying with the fact that not only have you died to sin—the old nature, unrighteousness, and your old lifestyle—but you have also been resurrected to a new way of life. You are a new creature that has been set free to walk in the newness of life (see Romans 6:4). This is just a little of what water baptism accomplishes.

Baptism of the Holy Spirit. This baptism empowers

us not just to live the life but to have the power for God to use us to share the gospel with others as well as equipping us for service. These three are the initial foundation stones that must be laid in the life of every Christian if they are going to be able to deal with these internal issues that we all struggle with.

Having laid these foundations, you can now begin the process of renewing your mind through God's word, which makes it possible for you to begin to experience victory in your life. You can enjoy what God has already accomplished for you in Christ, for His death already defeated all those conscious and unconscious bondages. Then you learn to walk in a new life empowered by the Holy Spirit that allows you to obey God's will as it is expressed through His Kingdom.

My hope is that as you read this book, you will realize the reason for your frustration after being born again is that you have not yet learned to allow the God who saved you and lives in you to take dominion over your thoughts and behaviors so that the fullness of His blessings can be released in and over your life. The goal is for us to be conformed to the image of Christ and that involves more than just being born again. It involves a life of service and sacrifice as we heed Jesus' words: "Then Jesus said to His disciples, 'If anyone desires to come after Me, let him deny himself, and take up his cross, and follow Me. For whoever desires to save his life will lose it, but whoever loses his life for My sake will find it'" (Matthew 16:24-25).

Pastor Louis Otey
Pittsburgh, PA
May 2020

CHAPTER
1

THE HUMAN CONDITION

I remember when I first received Jesus as my personal Savior. I thought, *Man, now I'm saved. This is the answer to my emptiness, pain, and heartaches. All my problems are over.* Perhaps you thought the same thing, but if you're like me, you have discovered that it's simply not true or that easy. People are preaching or believing a different Gospel than the one Jesus and the Apostles preached if that is the promise they are offering to people who surrender to the Lord.

Jesus did not say that being born again in and of itself was the answer to all of humanity's ills. Just because we stand up and say, "Jesus, come into my life and save me" is no guarantee that all our troubles are over. I refuse to mislead anyone into believing that if they agree to get saved, everything from then on will be peaches and cream. As much as I want to see people come to Christ, they must know the truth about the commitment they are being asked to make.

Listen to me. No one can guarantee if you get saved that your marriage, children, health, finances, or anything else will be taken care of. Jesus never preached that the born again experience was a panacea, a cure for all the ills of people. For some reason, we are afraid to preach the Gospel the way Jesus did. Many are afraid to tell people the truth because we think that the truth will take away from the attractiveness of the Gospel, and the truth of the matter is that it will. Look at what Jesus said in Matthew 10:34-39:

> "Do you suppose that I have come to bring peace to the earth. I did not come to bring peace, but a sword. For I have come to turn a man against His father, a daughter against her mother, a daughter-in-law against her mother-in-law a man's enemies will be the members of his own household. Anyone that loves his father or mother more than me is not worthy of me; anyone who loves his son or daughter more than me is not worthy of me; and anyone who does not take His own cross and follow me is not worthy of me. Anyone who finds his life will lose it, and who ever loses his life for my sake will find it" (NIV).

That's why unsaved wives can't get along with their saved husbands because they are no longer on the same page. They are serving two different masters; they are in two different kingdoms. That's why saved daughters can't get along with their unsaved mothers because they have two different philosophies of life. That's why a saved mother-in-law can't get along with an unsaved daughter-in-law because one is of God and the other is of the devil, one is of the light while the other is of the darkness. That's also why two Christians can't get along together if one is carnally-minded and one is spiritual.

There is no doubt that Jesus came to create a line or division between those who are His and those who are not His.

If you as a Christian can get along with the world, if you feel at home and comfortable with those who are not of Christ, you had better check yourself, for the Scriptures make it clear that friendship with the world makes you an enemy of God. If you are loved by those who are in the world, remember what the Word says: "The world would love its own" (John 15:19). Jesus will take second place to no one.

This is the reason that no one can make the promise that if you get born again, all your troubles will be over. No one can promise everything will be better, you'll love everybody, you'll have good health, you'll have money, houses, land, peace of mind, joy, a happy marriage, your children will be good boys and girls, everyone in the church will love you, and you won't have problems with drugs, alcohol, or lust. You see what we try to do? We paint this beautiful picture and create a wonderful dream that turns into a nightmare, a masterpiece of art that turns out to be worthless.

People eventually find out that even though they have made the decision to be born again, they are still experiencing emptiness, failure, pain, divorce, alcoholism, drug addiction, gluttony, sickness, death, lust for women or men, homosexual desires, greed, hate, and a whole lot more. *What is going on here? Will someone stop this religious illusion and let me out?* That's the cry in Christendom. *Will someone please tell the truth?* We have gotten caught going round and round on a merry-go-round, but never coming to the truth or finding an answer. *Well, what is the answer?* you may ask. *What's the cure-all for the panacea?*

Let's get something straight. I'm not speaking from a position of self-righteousness. The last thing I want to do is have you think I'm perfect or have all the answers. I have struggled with many of the problems I've described earlier. I know what it's like to experience failure, insecurity, marital challenges, and physical problems. I know what it's like to struggle with lust, to experience emptiness, to fight the urge to commit suicide. I have been there, too.

I can identify with what you may be experiencing if

you believed that all will be well—but it isn't. I know what it's like to pretend that everything's all right because you don't want to make a bad confession. I know what it's like not to be able to talk to people and tell someone what's going on for fear that they will lose respect for me because I am a preacher, a leader in the church, or a mature believer. After all, I am supposed to have it all together. Therefore, I pretended that everything was just fine and dandy while inside I was dying.

Because you're saved, you have to make people think that your life is perfect since Jesus came in. *Look at me world, I've been set free!* And then when you're alone, you deal with the sad reality that you're bound and you know it but you can't say a word about it. *What will people think of me?* You go on living in your own little nightmare and learn to lead a double life. In the church or at work, you put on a good-little-happy-overcoming-victory-Christian act with a phony little smile. Then when alone you cry, you're in pain, you hurt, and you're in despair. No wonder people throw their hands up in disgust saying, *I just can't live this. Why can't I be like everyone else who seems so happy?*

The sad part is that people believe us when we say to a man or woman trying to keep his or her marriage together, "Just get born again and God will heal your marriage," only to see after he or she gets born again that their spouse divorces them. We say to a family with a loved one racked with cancer, "You just get born again and God will heal them," only to see them die. We say to someone whose business is going down, "Just get born again and God will prosper you," only to see them lose everything. And then we sit back and wonder why people have become disillusioned and angry with God and the Church. We have misrepresented the purpose of the born again experience. I have come to call this the Born Again Panacea Syndrome; the belief that the born again experience in and of itself is the cure for everything wrong in life.

Now I want to state emphatically that I believe in the

born again experience. As stated earlier, however, there are scores of born again believers who are disillusioned, confused, and frustrated, constantly struggling with the human condition—not always because they don't want to live a holy life but because they lack understanding and the power to do so. The Bible says, "My people are destroyed for lack of knowledge" (Hosea 4:6). Let's get started by first laying the foundation for a proper and accurate understanding of the born again experience, which is the starting point for a relationship with the Lord.

CHAPTER
2

YOU MUST BE
BORN AGAIN

Let's see if we can find an answer to our tendency to believe that the born again experience is the answer to all our problems, or what I refer to as the Born Again Panacea Syndrome. What better place to begin than the words of Jesus in John 3:1-5:

> There was a man of the Pharisees named Nicodemus, a ruler of the Jews. This man came to Jesus by night and said to Him, "Rabbi, we know that You are a teacher come from God; for no one can do these signs that You do unless God is with him." Jesus answered and said to him, "Most assuredly, I say to you, unless one is born again, he cannot see the kingdom of God." Nicodemus said to Him, "How can a man be born when he is old? Can he enter a second time into his mother's

womb and be born?" Jesus answered, "Most assuredly, I say to you, unless one is born of water and the Spirit, he cannot enter the kingdom of God.

Let's get straight to the point. What was Jesus attempting to help Nicodemus understand? First, Nicodemus recognized that there was something special about the ministry of Jesus. People's lives were being changed and not just in a superficial way. He saw that the sick were healed, the dead were raised, the blind were made to see, the deaf were made to hear, and the leper was cleansed. Sinners were being forgiven and told to go and sin no more. As a result of coming into contact with Jesus, their lives were changed significantly.

He saw Jesus take twelve unlearned men and make them into students of His revolutionary teaching. He saw them also manifest the wonderful works of God as Jesus directed them to go and proclaim God's kingdom. He listened to Jesus teach the Scriptures in a way that both liberated and excited the listeners. He watched how people were motivated to follow Him. He listened as Jesus confounded the religious leaders who tried to trip him up.

After seeing the signs and wonders and after hearing the teachings, Nicodemus came to the conclusion that He had to be of God, for no one could do these things unless God was with Him. In a sense, Nicodemus wanted to know, *How do you do it? How do you take broken lives and make them whole?*

Nicodemus was also a teacher, but he had not experienced any of the miraculous results he had witnessed. Jesus, knowing the hearts of all men, heard from the heart of Nicodemus what his lips failed to convey. Jesus began to reveal to Nicodemus not just a method to bring about miracles, but He gave him that which is the answer to all of life's ills. It's the answer to the high drug and alcohol problems in our society. It's the answer to the high divorce rates, gang violence, and ongoing wars. It's the answer to the torn, broken, bitter, and lust-driven lives people lead. Notice what Jesus said: "Except a man is born again, he cannot see the Kingdom of God."

What was Jesus pointing to? He was pointing to the kingdom of God. Except one is born again, he cannot see it because he is blind to it. We see that the born again experience is what allows us to see the answer by lifting the blinders off our spiritual eyes so we can clearly see the kingdom of God. This is why you must be born again. Without this life-giving, eye-opening experience, one is left to stumble in darkness without hope, without light, and without any sense of direction whatsoever.

To understand the vital importance of the born–again experience, one must first become acquainted with the wonderful and glorious beginning of the human race, as well as the subsequent heart-breaking, life-draining, soul-corrupting Fall into sin, death, and depravity. Mankind was created to be inhabited by God so the two of them could commune together as well as rule over all God had created. Let's for a moment look back through the portal of time and see from God's perspective the reason we human beings are in the position we are in today.

After God had created Adam from the dust or clay of the earth, the Scripture says that He blew into him the breath of life and man became a living soul. Then we read in Genesis 2:15-17, "Then the Lord God took the man and put him into the garden of Eden to cultivate it and keep it. The Lord God commanded the man, saying, 'From any tree of the garden you may eat freely; but from the tree of the knowledge of good and evil you shall not eat, for in the day that you eat from it you will surely die'" (NASB). There is the crux of the problem: "In the day you eat from it, the day you rebel against My command, you will die." Man's death occurred as a result of disobeying God, the One who created him, the one who gave him life, the one who loved, cared, and provided for him and his wife.

Jesus informed us that Satan's (the serpent's) mission was and is to steal, kill, and destroy (see John 10:10). It has always been and continues to be. When Adam sinned, he became the servant of sin and at that point, sin killed his human spirit, corrupted his soul (mind, will, and emotions), and began to destroy his physical body. That meant man's soul was in rebellion, his spirit was dead, and his body dying. Where there was once harmony and peace with God, there was hostility against God. Where there was communion between man's spirit and God's spirit, there was silence and separation. Where the glory of God once covered the body of man, there was nakedness and shame. Even though man is the creation of God, Satan began to rule in man's heart at the point of the offence. Ephesians 2:1-3 says,

> And you were dead in your trespasses and sins, in which you formerly walked according to the course of this world, according to the prince of the power of the air, the spirit that is now working in the sons of disobedience. Among them, we too all formerly lived in the lust of our flesh, indulging the desires of the flesh and of the mind and were by nature children of wrath even as the rest (NIV).

Adam's sin ushered in the kingdom of darkness through which death began to reign. Romans 5:14 further explains, "Nevertheless death reigned from Adam until Moses, even over those who had not sinned in the likeness of the offence of Adam, who is a type of Him who was to come."

Earlier in Romans, Paul made us acutely aware of the fact that Adam did not just open the door to sin and death, but rather he himself became the door through which sin and death entered by corrupting all of creation: "Therefore, just as through one man sin entered the world, and death through sin, and thus death spread to all men, because all sinned" (Romans 5:12). So then, Adam became the opposite of what Jesus was and is. Adam was the door to death while Jesus is the door to life. Three things happened when Adam fell:

1. Sin was imputed,

2. Death was imparted.

3. The glory of God departed.

God was forced to vacate the spirit of man, bringing about spiritual death. For just as the physical body is dead without the human spirit, so the human spirit is dead without the Spirit of God inhabiting it. When God by his Spirit withdrew His indwelling presence from the spirit of man, the very life of man departed, leaving his spirit lifeless and dormant. It was at this point that the eyes of Adam and Eve were opened. For the very first time, they saw each other through the eyes of flesh and beheld one another as being naked, no longer clothed in God's glory. God's glory had departed and as a result, shame came upon them.

There we have the reason that one must be born again because until someone receives the life-giving Spirit of Christ, they are doomed, separated from God, and destined to everlasting torment in hell. Now that we have seen the purpose of the born again experience, we see that it is only the first step that one must take in order to see what God is after. The Bible makes it clear in Second Corinthians 4:3-4 that "if our Gospel be hid, it is hid to them that are lost: In whom the god of this world (Satan) hath blinded the minds of them which believe not, lest the light of the glorious gospel of Christ, who is the image of God, should shine unto them" (KJV).

If we carefully examine the experiences of the disciples, we find that it was not until *after* they had an encounter with the resurrected Christ that they indeed believed He was the Son of God. We see Thomas' unwillingness to believe that Jesus was raised from the dead, but if we examine the Scriptures, it becomes abundantly clear that not one of the disciples believed He truly was who He said he was. Even after seeing all the miracles, healings, raising the dead, multiplying food, and casting out demons, not one of them expected Jesus to rise from the dead.

Isn't it mind boggling how humanity could come face to face with divinity and yet not recognize that they were in the presence of the One who is the essence and substance of life? He is the one who has all the answers to every problem that harasses the human race. It's frightening to think that we could be in the midst of a visitation from God and yet not know it because our minds have been veiled and blinded.

When Jesus was about to make His triumphal entry down the Mount of Olives riding on a colt, and people were spreading their garments on the ground for the colt to walk on, "the whole multitude of the disciples began to praise God joyfully with a loud voice for all the miracles which they had seen, saying, Blessed is the King who comes in the name of the Lord; Peace in heaven and glory in the highest!" (Luke 19:37-38 NAS). In the midst of all of the celebration and rejoicing, they had no idea who was really in their presence. Luke 19:39-44 makes this clear:

> And some of the Pharisees called to Him from the crowd, "Teacher, rebuke Your disciples." But He answered and said to them, "I tell you that if these should keep silent, the stones would immediately cry out." Now as He drew near, He saw the city and wept over it, saying, "If you had known, even you, especially in this your day, the things that make for your peace! But now they are hidden from your eyes. For days will come upon you when your enemies will build an embankment around you, surround you and close you in on every side, and level you, and your children within you, to the ground; and they will not leave in you one stone upon another, because you did not know the time of your visitation."

From that passage, we learn that they were visited by the omnipotent and omniscient God of creation and yet they were as blind as bats. Not only were the Pharisees blind but every other person present was blind as well, even those who were singing and praising God, for none had any idea what they were saying, singing, or doing. They had no real understanding or insight as to who was on that colt. For the same crowd who cried "Hosanna! Blessed is the King" became the crowd that screamed for Him to be crucified.

They thought they were ushering in an earthly king who would establish an earthly kingdom and deliver them from Roman rule, when in reality they were ushering in the King of kings who would deliver their souls from the kingdom of darkness. Due to the fact that they had not been attentive or knowledgeable of the things of God, they did not recognize the time of their visitation.

Isn't it something that these same people who were praising God were as blind as the ones trying to find fault? The sad reality is that even those who knew Him best did not really believe or comprehend the message He was proclaiming. John 20:1-3 reports,

> Now the first day of the week Mary Magdalene went to the tomb early, while it was still dark, and saw that the stone had been taken away from the tomb. Then she ran and came to Simon Peter, and to the other disciple, whom Jesus loved, and said to them, "They have taken away the Lord out of the tomb, and we do not know where they have laid Him." Peter therefore went out, and the other disciple, and were going to the tomb.

When Mary Magdalene, Mary the mother of James, and Salome brought spices to anoint the body of Jesus, they were not expecting to find a resurrected Christ. They were expecting to find the lifeless, cold, rigor-mortis-affected body of Jesus. It's clear that when Mary went to the tomb and found the stone rolled away, her first thought was not *He has risen from the dead*. Her mind did not immediately go back to when Jesus said that He would be raised from the dead. Joy did not fill her heart as she realized her Redeemer's words were coming to pass. Her first thought was, *Someone has taken the Master's body and hidden it.*

They were in hot pursuit of a dead Jesus. The last thing on their minds was that He had risen from the dead like He said he would. This tells us that even though they walked with Him, lived, and ministered to, with, and on behalf of

Him, they were still blind and unable to really understand Him. Their minds were yet veiled.

When Mary brought news of the disappearance of the body of Jesus to the disciples, Peter ran to the tomb as fast as he could. When he arrived, he found the linen wrappings and the face cloth rolled up. When Peter and the other disciples went into the tomb and found this, they still did not believe He had been raised from the dead but they did believe something had happened: "Then the other disciple, who came to the tomb first, went in also; and he saw and believed. For as yet they did not know the Scripture, that He must rise again from the dead" (John 20:8-9).

They believed He was still dead and His body had been stolen out of the tomb because they did not understand the Scriptures that he must rise again. This is further evidence that their minds were yet blinded and void of understanding, even though they had walked with Him. Remember, this is the same Peter who when asked by Jesus, "But who do you say that I am?" responded by declaring, "Thou art the Christ" (Mark 8:29 KJV). Then look at how things begin to change. John 20:11-13 tells us,

> But Mary stood outside by the tomb weeping, and as she wept she stooped down and looked into the tomb. And she saw two angels in white sitting, one at the head and the other at the feet, where the body of Jesus had lain. Then they said to her, "Woman, why are you weeping?" She said to them, "Because they have taken away my Lord, and I do not know where they have laid Him."

After she had said this, she turned around and beheld Jesus standing there, but did not know it was Jesus.

> Jesus said to her, "Woman, why are you weeping? Whom are you seeking?" She, supposing Him to be the gardener, said to Him, "Sir, if you have carried Him away, tell me where you have laid Him, and I will take Him away" (John 20:15).

Notice she did not recognize who He was because her mind was still veiled because of unbelief. Look at verse John 20:16-17: "Jesus said to her, "Mary!" She turned and said to Him, "Rabboni!" (which is to say teacher)." Jesus said to her, "Do not cling to me, for I have not yet ascended to My Father; but go to my brethren and say to them, 'I am ascending to My Father and your Father, and to My God and your God."

Mary's back was turned away from Jesus when she first heard Him say, "Why are you weeping?" When He called her name, she turned around and had a face-to-face encounter with the resurrected Christ and immediately she recognized who He was. All of a sudden, it became clear. The veil was removed, and she believed. Why? She believed because of the encounter she had, not with the historic Christ, but with the resurrected Christ.

Up to this experience with Jesus, she only knew Him after the flesh. She knew Him as the Son of Man and a prophet of God. At the tomb for the first time, her eyes were opened and she saw Him as the Son of God. She saw and understood that He truly was the Christ. She came to know Him after the Spirit and not only after the flesh.

Many people know Jesus as the historic Christ who was a man claiming to be the Son of God. They know of the miracles attributed to Him. They know of the great messages He delivered and are acquainted with Him according to the flesh. All that doesn't change anything or make a difference in someone's life.

It's not until someone has a face-to-face encounter with the resurrected Christ that their eyes are opened. Only then will the veil be lifted that one might see the glorified face of Christ and be saved. It wasn't until Mary had a face-to-face, heart-to-heart encounter with the resurrected Christ that she believed and her eyes were opened. Second Corinthians 3:13-14 says,

> And are not as Moses, who use to put a veil over
> his face that the sons of Israel might not look

intently at the end of what was fading away. But their minds were hardened; for until this very day at the reading of the old covenant the same veil remains unlifted, because it is removed in Christ (NIV).

Up until this time, all of Israel had a veil over their minds that kept them from seeing. All they could understand was the Old Covenant, but Jesus had come to establish a New Covenant, yet they could not see it because of the veil. The veil can only be removed when someone is in Christ. Not only did Mary experience this, but every one of the disciples who Jesus appeared to had the same experience. It wasn't until He appeared to His disciples after His resurrection that they too believed. Even though they heard it from the lips of Mary, they did not believe until they had their own experience:

> Mary Magdalene came and told the disciples that she had seen the Lord, and that He had spoken these things to her. Then, the same day at evening, being the first day of the week, when the doors were shut where the disciples were assembled, for fear of the Jews, Jesus came and stood in the midst, and said to them, "Peace be with you." When He had said this, He showed them His hands and His side. Then the disciples were glad when they saw the Lord. So Jesus said to them again, "Peace to you! As the Father has sent Me, I also send you." And when He had said this, He breathed on them, and said to them, "Receive the Holy Spirit" (John 20:18-22)

When He breathed on them and said, "Receive the Holy Spirit," it was at that precise moment when they were born again, regenerated, and given new life. They were then new creatures in Christ. Let your mind go back to what Jesus said in Luke 19:42 as he made His entry into Jerusalem down the Mount of Olives:

"Would that you had known personally, even at least in this your day, the things that make for peace (for freedom from all the distresses that are experienced as the result of sin and upon which your peace—your security, safety, prosperity, and happiness—depends)! But now they are hidden from your eyes" (AMP).

His desire was that they would personally know the things that make for peace. Notice He said the *things* that make for peace He didn't say the *thing*. He also said it was hidden from them.

Therefore, we see that it wasn't simply the born again experience that they needed to have a full encounter with Christ. They need to know Him as the resurrected Lord who had all authority over life and death. Let's look in the next chapter and identify those things to which Jesus was referring that are necessary for an abundant life.

CHAPTER
3

THE KINGDOM
OF GOD

We must realize that if we are truly going to experience peace in every area of our lives, it begins with first having a face-to-face encounter with the Prince of peace. This will result in us being born again, causing the veil to be removed from our eyes so we can see Him and ourselves as He and we really are, so that peace can be lavished on us through the establishment of His Kingdom in our hearts.

Now the Bible says we must be born again: "Except a man be born again, he cannot see the *kingdom* of God" (John 3:3). Let's take a look at this word *kingdom*. The word for *kingdom* in the Greek is the word *basilea* and it means the rule, dominion, or reign of God, or more simply the government of God. Coming into God's kingdom speaks of surrendering, of being completely taken over by and submitting to God. It is the state of a submitted heart to

God. Another way to say it is that when you enter God's Kingdom, you come under the Lordship of Christ.

Jesus came proclaiming that God's kingdom had arrived and He was the embodiment of it. Jesus said, "Seek ye first the kingdom of God and his righteousness and all these things shall be added unto you" (see Matthew 6:33 KJV). As people surrender to the Lordship of Christ, they will begin to act like and resemble Him in every way. It is important to understand that Paul himself talks about Christians becoming complete or perfect in Christ, meaning that they would reach a state of maturity. The purpose of the kingdom of God is to cause us to recognize our need for God to be in charge of our lives and to seek His help through the Spirit to obey Him. That can only take place as we seek for God to rule and reign in our lives.

How is one to do that? It is done by pleading with God to take dominion over us. God's rule over me breaks and conquers me. This must be our intense desire; we cannot become satisfied living a life that is not under the influence and direction of the Holy Spirit. Jesus told His disciples in Matthew 6:31-33,

> "Therefore do not worry, saying, 'What shall we eat?' or 'What shall we drink?' or 'What shall we wear?' For after all these things the Gentiles seek. For your heavenly Father knows that you need all these things. But seek first the kingdom of God and His righteousness, and all these things shall be added to you."

In other words, Jesus was saying that if we would concentrate on coming under God's rule and dominion, He would take care of everything else we need. Notice He said *seek*, which means to have a holy lust to the point that we would not be satisfied with anything less than God having total control of our lives.

When people make God's Kingdom their pursuit in life, He has promised He would take care of everything else.

The Bible teaches that the Kingdom of God is not "eating and drinking, but righteousness and peace and joy in the Holy Spirit" (Romans 14:17). These benefits, those things that we desperately crave like joy or peace, can only be experienced as we seek for God to take control of our lives and then bring *everything* into alignment with His will.

Let me repeat. Jesus told Nicodemus, "Except a man be born of water and of the Spirit, he cannot enter into the kingdom of God. That which is born of the flesh is flesh; and that which is born of the Spirit is spirit" (John 3:5-6). In those words, we see both the keys to God's kingdom and the foundations necessary for anyone to experience the kingdom of God in their lives. As we search through the Scriptures, it becomes clear that when someone is born again, it is only the first key or foundation stone for that person to be brought under the governmental control of the Spirit of God, or to come under the dominion of God—His rule and reign.

Notice that Jesus said, "Except a man is born of water and the Spirit he cannot enter the Kingdom of God." These are the two other keys: water baptism and the baptism of the Holy Spirit. While I do not believe in baptismal regeneration, meaning that we are given new life only after or through water baptism, I do believe a biblical baptismal experience is a necessary foundation stone that will bring us under God's governmental control. There is more than just a ceremonial statement being made when someone is baptized in water. It is a supernatural experience whereby our heart is being circumcised and prepared to follow and obey God.

The first key to the Kingdom and a necessary foundation to the Kingdom is that we must be born again. The second is that we must be baptized in water, and the third is that one needs to experience the baptism of the Holy Spirit. If you look at the pattern we have in Scripture, you see these three foundation stones are laid all throughout the book of Acts.

First, a person gets saved, and then baptized in water, and then filled with the Holy Spirit. Salvation is always first and then the other two experiences, although they do not always occur in the same order. This is repeated all through the book of Acts because the apostles understood the necessity of starting people off right. Paul described his role in the church with these words: "As a wise master builder I have laid the foundation, and another builds on it" (1 Corinthians 3:10). If the foundation of a Christian's life is properly laid, they will be able to go through anything that life may bring and survive. Once the foundation of a house is secure, then one can build on top of that foundation with confidence it will support it.

These foundation stones are so important that it is necessary for us to slow down and spend a bit more time looking at each one of them in more detail. Let's start with water baptism in the next chapter.

CHAPTER
4

WATER
BAPTISM

I mentioned some of the reasons for and benefits of water baptism in the last chapter. Let's take a closer look at the significance of water baptism in the life of a believer in this chapter. Paul wrote in Colossians 2:11-12,

> In him you were also circumcised with a circumcision not performed by human hands. Your whole self ruled by the flesh was put off when you were circumcised by Christ, having been buried with him in baptism, in which you were also raised with him through your faith in the working of God, who raised him from the dead (NIV).

Here we learn that baptism in water is where and when the heart of a person is circumcised and he or she actually receives the sign of the New Covenant. It is at this point that the sinful nature is severed or cut away from the heart of the believer, which is the spiritual result of circumcision.

The sign of the first covenant was physical, having to do with the cutting away of the foreskin of the penis eight days after birth. This caused the Jews to put their confidence in the flesh because they were the covenant children of God, bearing the sign in their bodies. Under the New Covenant, we don't put our confidence in the flesh. Paul wrote in Philippians 3:3, "For we are the true circumcision, who worship in the Spirit of God and glory in Christ Jesus and put no confidence in the flesh" (NASB).

The false circumcision involves those who boast that they are covenant children because they carry in their own bodies the evidence of circumcision, the sign of the Old Covenant. The sign of the New Covenant, however, is circumcision of the heart, which cannot be seen in one's body but rather in one's lifestyle and attitudes. It is seen in how we handle or control our flesh, and in how we live our lives. Colossians 2:13-14 states,

> When you were dead in your sins and in the uncircumcision of your sinful nature, God made you alive with Christ. He forgave us all our sins, having cancelled the written code, with its regulations, that was against us and stood oppose to us; he took it away, nailing it to the cross (NIV).

In this passage, we clearly see that we are not saved by water baptism, but we are first made alive or born again with Christ through His presence living within us, while we are still uncircumcised fully, having our sinful nature attached to our heart. Circumcision of the heart is a separate, supernatural experience from salvation that occurs only when someone is baptized in water. Let's take a look at the following passage in the Amplified Version:

> In Him also you were circumcised with a circumcision not made with hands, but in a [spiritual] circumcision [performed by] Christ by stripping off the body of the flesh (the whole corrupt, carnal

nature with its passions and lusts). **[Thus you were circumcised when] you were buried with Him in [your] baptism,** in which you were also raised with Him [to a new life] through [your] faith in the working of God [as displayed] when He raised Him up from the dead. And you who were dead in trespasses and in the uncircumcision of your flesh (your sensuality, your sinful carnal nature), [God] brought to life together with [Christ], having [freely] forgiven us all our transgressions, Having cancelled and blotted out and wiped away the handwriting of the note (bond) with its legal decrees and demands which was in force and stood against us (hostile to us). This [note with its regulations, decrees, and demands] He set aside and cleared completely out of our way by nailing it to [His] cross (Colossians 2:11-14, emphasis added).

Here it is plain to see that we were circumcised when we were baptized. Coming out of the water symbolized our resurrection unto a new life, having been set free from the encumbrance of the sinful nature. Before we were born again, we were dead to God and alive to sin and the sinful nature, but after being born again, we die to the flesh and sin and must bury that old person along with its sinful nature.

The early Christians recognized the importance of water baptism, which is why every time we read of someone getting saved, they were immediately baptized in water. Now let's take a look at some examples in Scripture. When the church was first established during the outpouring of the Holy Spirit on the day of Pentecost, Peter explained and validated what they were experiencing concerning the manifestation of the Holy Spirit with the accompanying evidence of speaking in tongues. He then began to use that as a springboard to preach the Gospel concerning Jesus in Acts 2:22-38:

"Men of Israel, hear these words: Jesus of Nazareth, a Man attested by God to you by miracles, wonders, and signs which God did through Him in your midst, as you yourselves also know—Him, being delivered by the determined purpose and foreknowledge of God, you have taken by lawless hands, have crucified, and put to death; whom God raised up, having loosed the pains of death, because it was not possible that He should be held by it.

"For David says concerning Him: 'I foresaw the Lord always before my face, For He is at my right hand, that I may not be shaken. Therefore my heart rejoiced, and my tongue was glad; Moreover my flesh also will rest in hope. For You will not leave my soul in Hades, nor will You allow Your Holy One to see corruption. You have made known to me the ways of life; You will make me full of joy in Your presence.'

"Men and brethren, let me speak freely to you of the patriarch David, that he is both dead and buried, and his tomb is with us to this day. Therefore, being a prophet, and knowing that God had sworn with an oath to him that of the fruit of his body, according to the flesh, He would raise up the Christ to sit on his throne, he, foreseeing this, spoke concerning the resurrection of the Christ, that His soul was not left in Hades, nor did His flesh see corruption. This Jesus God has raised up, of which we are all witnesses. Therefore being exalted to the right hand of God, and having received from the Father the promise of the Holy Spirit, He poured out this which you now see and hear.

"For David did not ascend into the heavens, but he says himself: 'The Lord said to my Lord, "Sit at My right hand, till I make Your enemies Your footstool.'" "Therefore let all the house of Israel know assuredly that God has made this Jesus, whom you crucified, both Lord and Christ."

Now when they heard this, they were cut to the heart, and said to Peter and the rest of the apostles, "Men and brethren, what shall we do?" Then Peter said to them, "Repent, and let every one of you be baptized in the name of Jesus Christ for the remission of sins; and you shall receive the gift of the Holy Spirit."

Here it becomes clear that Peter's intent was to use their experience of the outpouring of the Holy Spirit to drive home the point that Jesus was the Christ they crucified through the hands of godless men. Then he goes on to refer to the prophecy of David, showing that the one who David spoke of was indeed Jesus the Christ. Once they heard this, they were cut or pierced to the heart and wanted to know what they should do? In other words, *How can we become a part of what you, Peter, are describing?*

Peter responded with the first key and foundation stone to the kingdom of God: Repent! Why? He did so because repentance leads to salvation. In other words, he was saying to them the same thing Jesus said to Nicodemus: *You must be born again.* He used the first key and foundation stone of being born again to open up the first door to remove the blinders so they could see clearly their entrance to the kingdom of God. And then he used the second key, which was to be baptized in water, so they could be circumcised by cutting away and burying the sinful nature since they had their sins forgiven. Then the final key was that they could receive the gift of the Holy Spirit just as they had witnessed happening to those in the Upper Room. What we see here is the carrying out of what Jesus spoke to Nicodemus:

1. You must be born again.

2. You must be born of water or be baptized in water.

3. Then be born of the Spirit or baptized in the Spirit.

These are the keys Jesus gave to Peter when He said, "I will give you the keys of the kingdom of heaven" (Matthew 16:19). Peter used them to open the doors to the Kingdom or the dominion of God and three thousand walked in on Pentecost. As we go through the book of Acts, we will see this pattern repeated again and again because the leaders realized the importance of laying a solid foundation for these new disciples. Let us turn our attentions to Acts 8:4-12:

> Therefore those who were scattered went everywhere preaching the word. Then Philip went down to the city of Samaria and preached Christ to them. And the multitudes with one accord heeded the things spoken by Philip, hearing and seeing the miracles which he did. For unclean spirits, crying with a loud voice, came out of many who were possessed; and many who were paralyzed and lame were healed. And there was great joy in that city. But there was a certain man called Simon, who previously practiced sorcery in the city and astonished the people of Samaria, claiming that he was someone great, to whom they all gave heed, from the least to the greatest, saying, "This man is the great power of God." And they heeded him because he had astonished them with his sorceries for a long time. But when they believed Philip as he preached the things concerning the kingdom of God and the name of Jesus Christ, both men and women were baptized.

Again, we see men and woman who heard the gospel of Christ getting saved and immediately being baptized. Why? This occurred because they understood the necessity of this important key to the Kingdom and foundation of the faith. Next let's look at Acts 8:26-40:

> Now an angel of the Lord spoke to Philip, saying,

"Arise and go toward the south along the road which goes down from Jerusalem to Gaza." This is desert. So he arose and went. And behold, a man of Ethiopia, a eunuch of great authority under Candace the queen of the Ethiopians, who had charge of all her treasury, and had come to Jerusalem to worship, was returning. And sitting in his chariot, he was reading Isaiah the prophet. Then the Spirit said to Philip, "Go near and overtake this chariot."

So Philip ran to him, and heard him reading the prophet Isaiah, and said, "Do you understand what you are reading?" And he said, "How can I, unless someone guides me?" And he asked Philip to come up and sit with him. The place in the Scripture which he read was this: "He was led as a sheep to the slaughter; and as a lamb before its shearer is silent, so He opened not His mouth. In His humiliation His justice was taken away, And who will declare His generation? For His life is taken from the earth."

So the eunuch answered Philip and said, "I ask you, of whom does the prophet say this, of himself or of some other man?" Then Philip opened his mouth, and beginning at this Scripture, preached Jesus to him. Now as they went down the road, they came to some water. And the eunuch said, "See, here is water. What hinders me from being baptized?"

Then Philip said, "If you believe with all your heart, you may." And he answered and said, "I believe that Jesus Christ is the Son of God." So he commanded the chariot to stand still. And both Philip and the eunuch went down into the water, and he baptized him. Now when they came up out of the water, the Spirit of the Lord caught Philip away, so that the eunuch saw him no more;

and he went on his way rejoicing. But Philip was found at Azotus. And passing through, he preached in all the cities till he came to Caesarea.

Here we see the same pattern. Philip came upon a eunuch who was the treasurer for the Ethiopian queen. He was reading the prophet Isaiah but was unable to understand what he was reading. God directed Philip to his chariot to explain to the eunuch what he was reading. As a result, Philip was able to preach Jesus to him and when they had come to some water, the eunuch requested that he be baptized. Philip replied, "If you believe with all your heart," and the eunuch said, "I believe that Jesus is the son of God."

Here we have a profession of faith in Jesus as God leading to salvation, which qualified him to be baptized in water and have his heart circumcised. We see first the foundation of being born again and then the second foundation of water baptism.

I believe I have sufficiently made the case of the purpose of and need for a biblical water baptism experience. It is necessary to receive the sign of the New Covenant, which is the circumcision of the heart or the cutting away of the sinful nature from the heart. That it is accomplished through water baptism where the sinful nature is buried in a watery grave. When one is raised out of the water, it symbolizes being resurrected with Christ to live in the newness of life. Next, let's look more closely at what has come to be known as the baptism of the Holy Spirit.

CHAPTER
5

BAPTISM OF
THE HOLY SPIRIT

John the Baptist made this statement in Matthew 3:11: "I indeed baptize you with water unto repentance, but He who is coming after me is mightier than I, whose sandals I am not worthy to carry. He will baptize you with the Holy Spirit and fire." Clearly, we see this being fulfilled on the day the Church was established, that being the day of Pentecost. At that time, the Church was endued with power from on high to carry out the mission Christ had given to it. As we examine the Scriptures and the experiences of the early church, we see that there were three experiences the people had. First, they were born again; second, they were baptized in water; and third, they received the baptism of the Holy Spirit with the evidence of speaking in tongues.

> When the Day of Pentecost had fully come, they were all with one accord in one place. And suddenly

there came a sound from heaven, as of a rushing mighty wind, and it filled the whole house where they were sitting. Then there appeared to them divided tongues, as of fire, and one sat upon each of them. And they were all filled with the Holy Spirit and began to speak with other tongues, as the Spirit gave them utterance (Acts 2:1-4).

Here we see that when the believers were in the Upper Room on the day of Pentecost, the Holy Spirit filled them all and they began to speak in tongues as the Spirit gave them the utterance.

In the book of Acts, we see that just about every time believers were baptized in the Holy Spirit, they experienced the supernatural ability to speak in tongues. Let's take a look at some of these passages. In Acts 9, we see the conversion of Paul on the road to Damascus. He encountered Jesus, was blinded, and told to go to the city where he would receive further instructions. At that time, God gave Ananias a vision and told him to go and find Saul:

Now there was a certain disciple at Damascus named Ananias; and to him the Lord said in a vision, "Ananias." And he said, "Here I am, Lord." So the Lord said to him, "Arise and go to the street called Straight, and inquire at the house of Judas for one called Saul of Tarsus, for behold, he is praying. And in a vision he has seen a man named Ananias coming in and putting his hand on him, so that he might receive his sight." Then Ananias answered, "Lord, I have heard from many about this man, how much harm he has done to Your saints in Jerusalem. And here he has authority from the chief priests to bind all who call on Your name."

But the Lord said to him, "Go, for he is a chosen vessel of Mine to bear My name before Gentiles, kings, and the children of Israel. For I will show him how many things he must suffer for My name's sake." And Ananias went his way and entered the house; and laying his hands on him he said, "Brother Saul, the Lord Jesus, who appeared to you on the road as you came, has sent me that you may receive your sight and be filled with the Holy Spirit." Immediately there fell from his eyes something like scales, and he received his sight at once; and he arose and was baptized. So when he had received food, he was strengthened. Then Saul spent some days with the disciples at Damascus (Acts 9:10-17).

Here we see a reluctant disciple, Ananias, sent by God to pray for Saul to spell out His purpose to him and restore His sight. When Ananias prayed, Saul was filled with the Holy Spirit and then baptized in water. We see the three foundation stones laid: salvation, water baptism, and baptism or the infilling of the Holy Spirit. Some would say he didn't speak with tongues but even though it is not recorded here, we know Saul did speak in tongues because he wrote in the book of Corinthians that he spoke in tongues more than all of those to whom he was writing (see 1 Corinthians 14:18).

In Acts chapter 10, we have the story of Cornelius and his family being saved and filled with the Holy Spirit, after which they spoke in tongues as well:

There was a certain man in Caesarea called Cornelius, a centurion of what was called the Italian Regiment, a devout man and one who feared God with all his household, who gave alms generously to the people, and prayed to God always. About the ninth hour of the day he saw clearly in a vision an angel of God coming in and saying to him, "Cornelius!" And when he observed him, he was afraid, and said, "What is it, lord?"

So he said to him, "Your prayers and your alms have come up for a memorial before God. Now send men to Joppa, and send for Simon whose surname is Peter. He is lodging with Simon, a tanner, whose house is by the sea. He will tell you what you must do." And when the angel who spoke to him had departed, Cornelius called two of his household servants and a devout soldier from among those who waited on him continually. So when he had explained all these things to them, he sent them to Joppa (Acts 10:1-8).

Here we learn of a Gentile who gave alms and prayed to God regularly. Both he and his family were devout in their fear of God but were not yet saved or born again. God sent an angel to Cornelius in a vision and told him to go find out what he needed to do to be born again. At the same time, God was preparing Peter for what he was to do. In Acts 10:24-48, we see God did something that opened everyone's eyes to God's purpose for both Jews and Gentiles alike:

> And the following day they entered Caesarea. Now Cornelius was waiting for them, and had called together his relatives and close friends. As Peter was coming in, Cornelius met him and fell down at his feet and worshiped him. But Peter lifted him up, saying, "Stand up; I myself am also a man." And as he talked with him, he went in and found many who had come together. Then he said to them, "You know how unlawful it is for a Jewish man to keep company with or go to one of another nation. But God has shown me that I should not call any man common or unclean. Therefore I came without objection as soon as I was sent for. I ask, then, for what reason have you sent for me?"

> So Cornelius said, "Four days ago I was fasting until this hour; and at the ninth hour I prayed in my house, and behold, a man stood before me in bright clothing, and said, 'Cornelius, your prayer

has been heard, and your alms are remembered in the sight of God. Send therefore to Joppa and call Simon here, whose surname is Peter. He is lodging in the house of Simon, a tanner, by the sea. When he comes, he will speak to you.' So I sent to you immediately, and you have done well to come. Now therefore, we are all present before God, to hear all the things commanded you by God."

Then Peter opened his mouth and said: "In truth I perceive that God shows no partiality. But in every nation whoever fears Him and works righteousness is accepted by Him. The word which God sent to the children of Israel, preaching peace through Jesus Christ—He is Lord of all—that word you know, which was proclaimed throughout all Judea, and began from Galilee after the baptism which John preached: how God anointed Jesus of Nazareth with the Holy Spirit and with power, who went about doing good and healing all who were oppressed by the devil, for God was with Him. And we are witnesses of all things which He did both in the land of the Jews and in Jerusalem, whom they killed by hanging on a tree. Him God raised up on the third day, and showed Him openly, not to all the people, but to witnesses chosen before by God, even to us who ate and drank with Him after He arose from the dead. And He commanded us to preach to the people, and to testify that it is He who was ordained by God to be Judge of the living and the dead. To Him all the prophets witness that, through His name, whoever believes in Him will receive remission of sins.

While Peter was still speaking these words, the Holy Spirit fell upon all those who heard the word.

And those of the circumcision who believed were astonished, as many as came with Peter, because the gift of the Holy Spirit had been poured out on the Gentiles also. For they heard them speak with tongues and magnify God.

Then Peter answered, "Can anyone forbid water, that these should not be baptized who have received the Holy Spirit just as we have?" And he commanded them to be baptized in the name of the Lord. Then they asked him to stay a few days.

From this passage, we see clearly that a group of individuals were both saved and baptized in the Holy Spirit at the same time and then baptized in water immediately when Peter and his entourage realized that God had made salvation available to the Gentiles. They knew they were saved and filled with the Holy Spirit because they heard them speak in tongues just like Peter and those with him in the Upper Room had done. The Scripture says he commanded them to be baptized in water.

Here again we see the keys of the kingdom being deployed: salvation, baptism of the Holy Spirit, and baptism of water. This is the pattern we see throughout the book of Acts because it was necessary that these foundation stones be laid for the rule, reign, and dominion of God to take hold in their lives.

Because these foundation stones have not been laid in people's lives today, they struggle and are unable to experience the victory God wants His people to experience and walk out in the world. Therefore, I plead with you, if you have not had these experiences in your spiritual life to pursue them because without these foundational keys of the Kingdom, God cannot do certain things in your life because your lack of biblical spiritual foundations will lead to spiritual sinkholes. Paul said as a wise master builder, he had laid the foundation and another built on it—but let each see how he builds upon it (see 1 Corinthians 3:10). Once we have laid the foundation, it's time to begin building on the foundation. What better place to start than in our next chapter?

CHAPTER
6

TO BE THE
FRIEND OF GOD

Often, we hear people talk about God being their friend; in fact, I have even referred to God as my friend when talking to others. We sing songs about being the friend of God: "He walks with me and talks with me and tells me I am his own." I wonder how many people really know what it is to be the friend of God? To answer this question, we must first understand what friendship is.

- Friendship is an earned privilege and not a right.

- It is the result of communion and fellowship.

- It involves being chosen or elected before the foundation of the world.

- It is characterized by two individuals opening up and revealing themselves to each other in an in-depth way. They share their hurts, joys, and secrets concerning the innermost recesses of their hearts.

Because friendship is based on trust born out of performance, the greater the trust, the greater the revelation of one's heart. As friendship relates to God, we must never assume because we are saved that we are automatically the friends of God. The terms *friendship* and *salvation* are not synonymous terms.

One can be brought into relationship with God through salvation and yet not be considered the friend of God. Salvation is an expression of God's love for us while friendship is a result of our proven love for God. It is extended to us only when through obedience we meet the conditions God has established. Salvation is the result of embracing the finished work of Christ. It requires no work or effort on our part. Jesus Himself does all the work and freely offers salvation as a gift.

Though it is a gift, it did not come cheaply, for it cost Jesus a great deal. It was because of the Father's love for us that Jesus freely laid down His life in order to purchase our salvation. We can do nothing to earn or merit it: "For the wages of sin is death, but the gift of God is eternal life in Christ Jesus our Lord" (Romans 6:23) and "for by grace you have been saved through faith, and that not of yourselves; it is the gift of God, not of works, lest anyone should boast" (Ephesians 2:8-9). Even the faith to embrace Christ as Savior did not originate with us but rather it was a gift from God—which brings us to the reality that salvation depends solely on Christ's obedience.

On the other hand, friendship is earned through our obedience. Jesus said to His disciples in John 15:14, "You are My friends if you do whatever I command you." Friendship is not a right but rather a privilege. True salvation cannot be lost but friendship can. Salvation has to do with relationship while friendship has to do with fellowship.

It is possible to be in relationship with God and not

be enjoying intimate fellowship with God, but we cannot enjoy fellowship with God apart from relationship. In order to obtain fellowship with God, one must first be brought into a relationship with God through salvation. It is as a result of one's obedience to God's word that friendship is offered and as a result of friendship, the character, integrity, love, and fruit of the Spirit are produced, out of which a true appreciation for God is developed. In order for us to experience all that God has for us, we must have a clear understanding of what *imputed* righteousness and *imparted* righteousness mean to the believer.

Imputed means to attribute (righteousness or guilt) as coming from another. In other words, this has to do with what God does for us. *Imparted* has to do with what God does in us or to us in order to conform us to the image of Christ. To gain a clearer understanding of these terms, let's look at the life of Samson. Keep in mind that the biblical pattern is first the natural and then the spiritual (see 1 Corinthians 15:46). What we are about to witness in the life of Samson is an Old Testament example of *imputed* and *imparted* righteousness. In the book of Judges 13:1-2, we read

> Again the Israelites did evil in the eyes of the Lord, so the Lord delivered them into the hands of the Philistines for forty years. A certain man of Zorah, named Manoah, from the clan of the Danites, had a wife who was childless, unable to give birth.

We see Israel being placed into the hands of the Philistines for a forty-year period because of their disobedience to God. At the end of their forty years of tribulation, God intervened by speaking to the wife of Manoah who was barren and had no children:

> Now there was a certain man from Zorah, of the family of the Danites, whose name *was*Manoah; and his wife *was* barren and had no children. And the Angel of the Lord appeared to the woman and said to her, "Indeed now, you are barren and

have borne no children, but you shall conceive and bear a son. Now therefore, please be careful not to drink wine or *similar* drink, and not to eat anything unclean. For behold, you shall conceive and bear a son. And no razor shall come upon his head, for the child shall be a Nazirite to God from the womb; and he shall begin to deliver Israel out of the hand of the Philistines (Judges 13:2-5).

We see that the angel of the Lord revealed to Manoah's wife that she was to bring forth a son, and that she was to pay special attention to what she ate and drank because the child would be a Nazirite from birth. What the angel actually instructed her to do was to make a Nazirite vow on behalf of her son. In Numbers 6:2-21 we read about a Nazirite vow along with the specifications for entering into one.

In this passage we read the instructions the angel of the Lord gave to Manoah's wife. She was expected to fulfill the Law of the Nazirite on behalf of Samson so he would be a Nazirite from the womb. Here we see an Old Testament type of a profound and wonderful truth that once we grasp it will totally liberate us from sin, guilt, and intimidation. Before we talk about New Testament revelation, it is important that we first understand what took place in regard to Samson.

First, Samson's mother heard and received the word of God from the angel of the Lord and fulfilled the Nazirite terms by fulfilling the law of the Nazirite until Samson was born. At the time of his birth, her obedience was *imputed* or written over to his account so Samson became a Nazirite from birth even though he did nothing to earn or merit it by his own works. It was the result of grace or unmerited favor and was a free gift not based on his obedience but rather on the obedience of his mother.

It was consummated and sealed by God at his birth and could never be broken by his mother or him. It was forever settled, and her obedience was transferred over to his account without his knowledge or approval. The only one who was capable of breaking the vow was his mother and she would have had to have broken it before he was born. Her vow became his vow, her obedience became his obedience, her consecration became his consecration, her anointing became his anointing, her righteousness became his righteousness.

Watch how this wonderful revelation unfolds. The name Manoah means rest; it is a type of the rest that people receive from God when they cease from their own works of trying to become righteous by doing good works. Manoah's wife was a type of Christ who fulfilled the law on our behalf because we were powerless and helpless. He became our representative by satisfying God's law through His obedience of death, at which time God imputed His righteousness to us.

The word Nazirite means to be separated, to consecrate, to set apart, to be sanctified. It is a type of our being born again and our positional sanctification. Samson means a ray of light, a type of us who once we are born again become children of light. When we put it all together, it looks like this. Our salvation is a result of our resting in God, by ceasing from our own works and totally relying on the finished work of Christ, who fulfilled the law of God by walking in total obedience to the law and will of God. He sanctified Himself in order that we would be sanctified. He became our representative and accomplished what we were unable to accomplish on our own.

As a result, His obedience, righteousness, sanctified life, and anointing were *imputed*, accounted, credited, written over, and deposited into our spiritual account when we were born again. Therefore, we come forth from our spiritual wombs sanctified, holy, sinless, anointed, and righteous, not based on our own obedience but based on His. It is a result of God's grace and had nothing to do with our obedience, but everything to do with his.

Just as Samson had a purpose and a calling in God before his conception and birth, we have the same holy calling before the foundation of the world. We see that Sampson was born a Nazirite not in the will of the flesh or man but rather according to the will of God, just as we are born again—not of the will of flesh or man but of God. Let's continue our discussion of *imputed* and *imparted* righteousness in the next chapter.

CHAPTER
7

THE LAW OF
THE NAZIRITE

We discussed in the last chapter the concept of *imputed* righteousness, which is righteousness bestowed on someone even though the actions of that righteousness were carried out by someone else. I used the example of Samson who was a Nazirite by birth through no choice or action of his own; it was because of his mother's decision and behavior. I want to go back and give a brief synopsis of the typology represented in Samson as it relates to our salvation. Let's take a look at the law of the Nazirite in Numbers chapter 6:1-9:

> Then the Lord spoke to Moses, saying, "Speak to the children of Israel, and say to them: 'When either a man or woman consecrates an offering to take the vow of a Nazirite, to separate himself to the Lord, he shall separate himself from wine and similar drink; he shall drink neither vinegar made

from wine nor vinegar made from similar drink; neither shall he drink any grape juice, nor eat fresh grapes or raisins. All the days of his separation he shall eat nothing that is produced by the grape-vine, from seed to skin.

'All the days of the vow of his separation no razor shall come upon his head; until the days are fulfilled for which he separated himself to the Lord, he shall be holy. Then he shall let the locks of the hair of his head grow. All the days that he separates himself to the Lord he shall not go near a dead body. He shall not make himself unclean even for his father or his mother, for his brother or his sister, when they die, because his separation to God is on his head. All the days of his separation he shall be holy to the Lord.

'And if anyone dies very suddenly beside him, and he defiles his consecrated head, then he shall shave his head on the day of his cleansing; on the seventh day he shall shave it"

These verses make it clear that anyone taking a Nazirite vow was to be holy unto the Lord. It was mandated that a person who took such a vow was to do nothing at all to make himself unclean.

As the story continues, we see that even though Samson had a great beginning, it was not long before he began to walk in carnality. He became an immoral man who was only out to fulfill the desires of his flesh. He walked in fornication; he defiled himself and his parents by eating honey from a dead lion's carcass that he had killed and in which later bees built a hive. He came along, ate the honey, and then gave it to his parents without telling them where he got it. He violated the law of the Nazirite on two points. First, they were not to eat an unclean animal, and a lion was considered unclean. Second, they could not eat an animal they had found dead.

By eating this honey, he broke the vow. Another way a Nazerite could break his vow was by being in the presence of dead people. If a dead body was to suddenly come in contact with a Nazirite, he would be considered unclean and the vow violated. That being the case, Samson broke his vow over a thousand times because in one fight alone he killed a thousand Philistines, not to mention all the other people and animals he killed. Yet he did not lose his anointing and here is why.

If Samson had taken a Nazirite vow the normal way, then the keeping or the breaking of that vow would have been dependent solely on him and his actions, which would have determined whether he kept his anointing. In other words, he would have had to perform works of obedience in order to maintain his consecrated position from whence came his anointing. A Nazirite was anointed for service based on his being consecrated [exclusively devoting himself to the worship of God] and sanctified [to set apart unto God for a divine purpose].

Once a Nazirite broke any portion of the Nazirite law, he ceased to be consecrated and sanctified and no longer qualified to be a Nazirite, thus forfeiting the anointing. The fact is, as stated earlier, his anointing was a result of his *imputed* righteousness, which is a type of the anointing we receive from Christ: "But the anointing which you have received from him abides in you" (1 John 2:27a).

We have an anointing that abides or permanently remains in us. Samson's anointing was permanent because it was a result of his mother's consecration. Because she consecrated and sanctified herself, God anointed her to fulfill the purpose he had set her apart to accomplish—which was to produce a Nazirite from birth. God took her anointing and transferred it over to Samson's account, just as Jesus' anointing was *imputed* to us.

When Jesus said in Luke 4:18, ""The Spirit of the Lord is upon Me, because He has anointed Me," that same anointing that was on Christ was assigned to us. He said in

John 17:19, "I sanctify myself that they may be sanctified by the truth." Along with that act of consecration came an anointing or unction for service, not to mention the fact that the book of Colossians 2:9-10 says, "For in Christ all the fullness of the Deity lives in bodily form, and in Christ you have been brought to fullness. He is the head over every power and authority" (NIV).

Notice all the fullness of the Godhead—Father, Son, and Holy Spirit—dwelt in the bodily form of Christ and the Bible says that if Christ dwells in you, you also have the same fullness of deity in you. Jesus is the Christ, the Anointed One. How can you help but be anointed when you have Christ dwelling and abiding permanently in you? When Jesus comes in, He brings His anointing with Him, and because He stays forever, so does his anointing.

Therefore, we never have to be intimidated by someone else's anointing because theirs is no greater than ours. If we are born again, we have the same anointing as Jesus, and we can't do any better or get any more than that. We can't lose it because we didn't earn it—Jesus did. He deposited it into your account so all you have to do is move in faith, expecting to be anointed because it abides in you forever. Just think, you are just as anointed today as Jesus was 2,000 years ago. You are just as anointed as Oral Roberts, Billy Graham, Fred Price, Bishop T. D. Jakes, or anyone else you can think of.

Therefore, you should never fill intimidated again. The only difference is the assignment God has given you to fulfill your purpose, but the anointing is equal to anyone else's anointing. I won't spend much time with the other type of righteousness, which is *imparted*. That is simply the grace work God does in you after your born again experience. It is the righteousness God grants you in response to obeying His word, imparted to you on a day-by-day basis. Your *imputed* righteousness, however, will never increase for the day you are born again is the day all the righteousness of Christ is *imputed* to you because of who He is and not because of what you have done.

Let's move on now to examine an important process of entering into the kingdom of God after being born again and that is dealing with the past so you can enjoy the present blessing of God.

CHAPTER
8

GHOST OF
THE PAST

It is sad that many who are the elect of God, meaning that they have been chosen to be saved and a part of the family of God before the foundations of the world, still live in personal defeat. Just being the elect does not guarantee in and of itself that we will live in personal victory, walking in the joy of the Lord. If we do not follow the prescribed plan God has described in His Word, we may be on our way to heaven yet not enjoying the ride—in the Kingdom yet not under the control of the King. We may not experience the excitement and joy of where we are going because we have not taken advantage of all the things provided for us to make the journey meaningful and enjoyable.

Many Christians find themselves in that very place— on their way to heaven yet not walking in the joy of the Lord or living under the influence of the Holy Spirit. They are walking in depression, fear, and confusion, their lives dominated by a passion for the things of the world and not for Christ. God has given us everything we need to be victorious in our personal lives, but we often have not taken advantage of what he has given us.

Many Christians may look happy, victorious, successful, and even excited about their future, but are in fact inwardly frightened because they are being haunted by ghosts. When they are alone, they find themselves falling into deep depression, so they are constantly seeking relationships that will make them feel better. Their plans for the future have been sabotaged, and they are unable to enjoy success because they are expecting something to go wrong. They are wondering what if this happens or that doesn't happen. They find it difficult to enjoy long-term relationships because they are thinking, *What do they really want from me?* The ghost of the past haunts them to the point that they fear the future. Some have sought help to no avail, while others are afraid to seek help lest someone think they are crazy.

We cannot allow the past to affect our future, nor can we deal with our past the same way psychology advises us to deal with it. If we use the approach of the world, we will spend more time chasing the ghosts of our past and will never truly overcome them so our present and future can unfold and move forward.

It is true to a large degree that we have been shaped by the experiences of our past, but that does not mean we have to remain prisoners of past failures. Those things that have occurred in the past are robbing us of true peace of mind, sabotaging relationships, and keeping us from enjoying any degree of success we may have experienced. The ghosts of our past can be frightening and terrifying adversaries. In fact, in the wrong hands they can be used as weapons of mass destruction against us, destroying any hope of peace, the enjoyment of spiritual and natural success, and the fulfillment of lasting relationships.

The sad reality is that not only can the screams and

shrieks of these ghosts affect our relationships with people, they can also affect our relationship with God. Because we are constantly looking back at a past relationship with an unloving and uncaring earthly parent, we are robbed of our ability to trust our heavenly Father.

We can never expect to successfully deal with the past by using the world's approach. We must understand how God deals with the past in contrast to how the world deals with it. The world deals with it by going back, digging it up, examining it, opening up old wounds, and reliving bad experiences. If an answer can't be found, we blame others for our problems.

The reason we in the church are unable to deal with it is because we have embraced the psychology of the world and have mixed it with the Bible. God never tells us to go back and reopen the past. Instead, He does away with it all together. If we use man's remedies, the past is always there taunting us, but in God's system, He brings finality to the past so it never affects us again.

God never says go back and reopen the past; He says leave it behind. Paul wrote, "...forgetting those things which are behind and reaching forward to those things which are ahead, I press toward the goal for the prize of the upward call of God in Christ Jesus" (Philippians 3:13-14). God deals with the past through death and resurrection: "If anyone is in Christ, he is a new creation; old things have passed away; behold, all things have become new" (2 Corinthians 5:17).

You must see yourself as having died to the old man or sinful nature to become a partaker of the divine nature of Christ. You, my friend, are not the same person that you were before your born again experience. You may look the same but on the inside, you are a new person with a new spiritual identity. You must see yourself as having died to your old lifestyle after being born again, free from the past. Sin no longer has dominion over you. That old person is dead! When you were baptized in water, it was buried.

You are no longer in Adam, but you are now in Christ,

so the Adamic nature no longer has power over you. Now what you must do is renew your mind so that you can establish new patterns of lifestyles to replace the old. Before you do, you are dealing with vestiges of your unrenewed mind, but now God has given you the mind of Christ. You must learn to think like Him by renewing your mind with His Word, teaching, and fellowship with other believers from whom you can learn. You must begin the process of renewing the mind, you have taken an important step after you have laid your foundation.

God has forgiven you for your past and has given you a new life in Christ, having completely set you free from the power of sin. Don't go back and revisit that past unless you are working with a spiritual counselor and the Spirit has directed you to address a particular issue. Once you address it and deal with it, let it go. Don't linger over its effects. Then change the way you act by changing the way you think.

It is time that you begin to see things from God's perspective. You must find out and understand who you really are now that you have this new life and comprehend what advantages it has given you. When you silence the ghosts of the past by finding out who you are and learning how to walk in that reality by renewing your mind is an important step once you have laid your foundation

I hope you are understanding what I mean by The Born Again Panacea. Coming to the Lord is not the end all of your spiritual journey; it is the first step. After that, you must lay a proper foundation and then move on to build a proper spiritual house that can weather the storms of life that have come, are here, and are yet to come. Let's move on to consider other steps to take like the one we described in this chapter that will help you fortify yourself against disillusionment and disappointment.

CHAPTER
9

STARTING
THE PROCESS

Colossians 3:1-10 states,

> If then you were raised with Christ, seek those things which are above, where Christ is, sitting at the right hand of God. Set your mind on things above, not on things on the earth. For you died, and your life is hidden with Christ in God. When Christ *who is* our life appears, then you also will appear with Him in glory.

> Therefore put to death your members which are on the earth: fornication, uncleanness, passion, evil desire, and covetousness, which is idolatry. Because of these things the wrath of God is coming upon the sons of disobedience, in which you yourselves once walked when you lived in them.

But now you yourselves are to put off all these: anger, wrath, malice, blasphemy, filthy language out of your mouth. Do not lie to one another, since you have put off the old man with his deeds, [1]and have put on the new *man* who is renewed in knowledge according to the image of Him who created him.

It is time to become heavenly minded once you have been resurrected from the grave of sin and death through baptism. You were dead to God but when you gave your life to Christ, you died to sin and became alive to Him. You have been translated from the kingdom of darkness into the Kingdom of light and His dear Son. Notice Paul said if you have been risen with Christ, you must change the way you think.

You can no longer think like a person who is dead in sin and bound by it. You must now see yourself the way God sees you. You are no longer in the kingdom of darkness being controlled by the sinful nature, Satan, and his demons, but you have been transferred out from under their rule. You no longer live by its principles, values, and regulations, but you must learn to live by heavenly, godly principles, rules, and regulations as you are empowered by the indwelling presence of the Holy Spirit. After living your old life with a worldly mindset seeking after carnal things that kept you deceived and in bondage, you must now be heavenly minded.

I have heard people say that Christians are so heavenly minded they can be no earthly good, but I have found the opposite of that to be true. Christians can be so earthly or worldly minded that they are no heavenly good. God can't use them because they think too much like the world and are always looking for what God can and should do for them as opposed to what they should do for God.

Notice we are told we must seek the things that are above. That word *seek* means to require, crave, or demand. You seek something when you need it, must have it, and won't be satisfied until you find it. What should we be seeking? First, His kingdom—His rule, reign, dominion, and Lordship over our lives. Jesus said to seek first the kingdom of God and His righteousness (see Matthew 6:33). Second, we seek our inheritance. Peter said we have an inheritance that is imperishable and undefiled and will not fade away. It is reserved in heaven for us who are protected by the power of God through faith for a salvation ready to be revealed in the last days.

Third, we seek heavenly blessings. Paul said in the book of Ephesians 1:3, "Blessed be the God and Father of our Lord Jesus Christ, who has blessed us with every spiritual blessing in the heavenly places in Christ." These are just some of the things we must begin to seek after.

We seek those things that are above because He has raised us up and seated us in heavenly places in Christ. When Christ was seated in heavenly places at the right hand of God the Father, He secured our place there because we were and are in Christ. I seek the things that are above because I am abiding and living in Christ Jesus, for it is in Him we live and move and have our being" (Acts 17:28). Based on that reality, why wouldn't we be seeking those things that are above?

Notice we must have the right mindset and be focused on those things that are above so we don't get distracted by the things that are earthly and can lead us astray, opening doors and giving the devil a place in our lives. Why should we seek these heavenly things? We should do so because we have died to sin and the old lifestyle and have a new eternal life hidden with Christ in God. This is a life we can never lose.

I may lose my joy, peace, and, for a while, my way, but Satan can never take my life, for it is hidden in a place he cannot reach. Jesus said that I am in the palm of my Father's hand and no man can pluck me out (see John 10:28-29). He who has the Son has life; he who has not the Son does not live life (see 1 John 5:12). Because of the fact that we are alive and in Christ, when He returns and is revealed in His Second Coming, we also will be revealed with Him in all His glory.

Now notice what Paul wrote. We should consider the members of our earthly body to be dead to immorality, impurity, passion, evil desire, and greed, which amounts to idolatry. In other words, based on the facts of all the other things he wrote in the preceding verses, we can consider ourselves dead to sin and its power, no longer under its control. That's because the old person is dead, and a new person has been born, free from sin and Satan's control.

Therefore, I can consider the members of my earthly body to be dead to sinful activity: "For you died, and your life is hidden with Christ in God" (Colossians 3:3). Then he instructed us to put aside anger, wrath, malice, slander, and abusive speech from our mouth and "do not lie to one another, since you have put off the old man with his deeds, and have put on the new man who is renewed in knowledge according to the image of Him who created him" (Colossians 3:9-10).

We now have the power to resist sinful activity and take off all the grave clothes of the old self and put on the new self, which is being conformed to the image of Christ. It won't be easy, which is the reason we must seek those things that are above, stay focused on heavenly things, renew our minds, study the Word, and be established in a Bible-believing and teaching church where we develop relationships with others who are like-minded so we might grow in our faith.

Now perhaps you understand why so many people assumed that being born again was the end all to their spiritual and life problems. Being born again is just the beginning. It is the gateway to a life of learning, sacrifice, and renewing the mind that takes us from where we were to where we need to be. This isn't magic and there are no shortcuts. The key to maturity in Him is to know what it is that only God can do so we then know what He expects from us—the things that only we can do. We read the Word, God quickens the meanings and helps us apply them to our situation, but if we don't read, He won't read for us—and He cannot speak through His Word to us. Then there is the matter of being in the Spirit, which we will discuss in the next chapter.

Chapter
10

UNDERSTANDING WHAT IT MEANS TO BE IN THE SPIRIT

If we are to understand and walk out these principles of our salvation, we must have a clear understanding of what it truly means to be in and walk in the Spirit. Jesus made a statement in John 4:23-24 that shows us why it is important to understand what is means to be in the Spirit:

> "But an hour is coming, and now is, when the true worshipers will worship the Father in spirit and truth; for such people the Father seeks to be His worshipers. God is spirit, and those who worship Him must worship in spirit and truth."

If God is seeking true worshippers who will worship Him in spirit and in truth, then it is important for us to know and understand what it means to worship God, to be in the Spirit, and to do it in truth. Here are some important things to understand as we seek to fulfill what Jesus said:

1. Let's define worship. It is composed of praise and obedience. Worship is the exaltation of God with obedience.

2. Praise is an element of worship but is not worship in and of itself.

3. Praise, when accompanied by obedience, equals worship.

4. One can praise without obedience, but one cannot worship God without obedience.

5. Praise is our acknowledgement of God's power, authority, wisdom, and worthiness. It does not require, look for, or receive a response from God.

Let's take a closer look at praise for a moment. Psalms 150 expresses just about everything you need to know about praise.

Praise the Lord!

Praise God in His sanctuary;
Praise Him in His mighty firmament!

Praise Him for His mighty acts;
Praise Him according to His excellent greatness!

Praise Him with the sound of the trumpet;
Praise Him with the lute and harp!
Praise Him with the timbrel and dance;
Praise Him with stringed instruments and flutes!
Praise Him with loud cymbals;
Praise Him with clashing cymbals!

Let everything that has breath praise the Lord.

Praise the Lord!

This psalm uses the word praise 13 times in six verses.

Verse one tells us where God is to be praised, which is everywhere. The next verses tell us why "for His mighty acts." Verses three through six tells us how, which is through music and dancing, and who is to praise, which is everyone and everything that has breath. Yet all this can be done without obedience to the truth of the Scriptures. It is possible to do all of this and not achieve worship. Jesus tells us, however, that God is looking for those who will worship Him in both spirit and truth.

Let's turn our focus to what it means to be in the spirit and in truth. It's important to point out that under the Old Covenant, people worshipped God in the flesh but in the limited truth of the Old Covenant. Under the New Covenant, we worship God in the spirit and in the truth of the New Covenant established by Christ. So then, what does it mean to be in the spirit? For the answer to this question, we must take a look at Romans 8:1-11 in which the Apostle Paul left no doubt as to what it means:

> There is therefore now no condemnation to those who are in Christ Jesus, who do not walk according to the flesh, but according to the Spirit. For the law of the Spirit of life in Christ Jesus has made me free from the law of sin and death. For what the law could not do in that it was weak through the flesh, God did by sending His own Son in the likeness of sinful flesh, on account of sin: He condemned sin in the flesh, that the righteous requirement of the law might be fulfilled in us who do not walk according to the flesh but according to the Spirit. For those who live according to the flesh set their minds on the things of the flesh, but those who live according to the Spirit, the things of the Spirit. For to be carnally minded is death, but to be spiritually minded is life and peace. Because the carnal mind is enmity against God; for it is not subject to the law of God, nor indeed can be. So then, those who are in the flesh cannot please God.

But you are not in the flesh but in the Spirit, if indeed the Spirit of God dwells in you. Now if anyone does not have the Spirit of Christ, he is not His. And if Christ is in you, the body is dead because of sin, but the Spirit is life because of righteousness. But if the Spirit of Him who raised Jesus from the dead dwells in you, He who raised Christ from the dead will also give life to your mortal bodies through His Spirit who dwells in you.

In the first verse, Paul lets us know that if we are in Christ, there is no condemnation or sentence of death on us. Therefore, we need not be concerned any longer about eternal punishment or experiencing the wrath of God. Why? It's because the law of the spirit of life in Christ has set us free from the law of sin and death. What does that actually mean? Paul answered that in 2 Corinthians 3:

But if the ministry of death, written and engraved on stones, was glorious, so that the children of Israel could not look steadily at the face of Moses because of the glory of his countenance, which glory was passing away, how will the ministry of the Spirit not be more glorious? For if the ministry of condemnation had glory, the ministry of righteousness exceeds much more in glory. For even what was made glorious had no glory in this respect, because of the glory that excels. For if what is passing away was glorious, what remains is much more glorious (2 Corinthians 3:7-11).

Notice he referred to the Ten Commandments as the ministry of death. What was written in letters and engraved on stone? It was the Law and the Law could only produce spiritual death with the consequences of eternal damnation in hell. It had no ability to restore life with God once it had been broken. Notice he wrote that the glory of God or His divine presence came with the Law when the commandments were given. The glory of God was seen by the shining of Moses' face, letting them know that God's presence was with Moses when he received the Ten Commandments.

Yet the glory of God began to fade because it was given through a covenant that would also fade away because the presence of God could not dwell eternally with and in the people under the Old Covenant that exposed the consequences of sin but with no power to wipe out or reverse the results. Therefore, Moses covered his face so that they could not see the fading of God's glory from his face.

The Bible tells us that the Law had become our tutor to lead us to Christ:

> But before faith came, we were kept under guard by the law, kept for the faith which would afterward be revealed. Therefore the law was our tutor to bring us to Christ, that we might be justified by faith. But after faith has come, we are no longer under a tutor. For you are all sons of God through faith in Christ Jesus. For as many of you as were baptized into Christ have put on Christ (Galatians 3:23-27).

So the law of the spirit of life in Christ is the law of faith. Paul added in Galatians 3:27-28, "Where is boasting then? It is excluded. By what law? Of works? No, but by the law of faith. Therefore we conclude that a man is justified by faith apart from the deeds of the law."

The Bible is clear that we are saved by grace through faith but not of ourselves for it is the gift of God less any man should boast (see Ephesians 2:9). We cannot take credit for this work of grace through faith for even the faith that saves us does not originate with us; it is the gift of God. The law of faith, which is the law of the spirit of life in Christ, has set us free from the judgment of the Law:

> For what the law could not do in that it was weak through the flesh, God did by sending His own Son in the likeness of sinful flesh, on account of sin: He condemned sin in the flesh, that the

righteous requirement of the law might be ful-filled in us who do not walk according to the flesh but according to the Spirit. For those who live according to the flesh set their minds on the things of the flesh, but those who live according to the Spirit, the things of the Spirit. For to be carnally minded is death, but to be spiritually minded is life and peace. Because the carnal mind is enmity against God; for it is not subject to the law of God, nor indeed can be. So then, those who are in the flesh cannot please God (Romans 8:3-8).

Now it is important to understand what it means to be in the flesh. It cannot be talking about being physically in the flesh because if that were true, Christ could not please God because He was physically present in flesh and blood. To be in the flesh here means to be in Adam—to be unre-generate and controlled in and by the sinful nature—rather than being in Christ where our new life is. If we are in Adam and controlled by the Adamic nature, it is impossible to please God. To be in the flesh in this instance is to be unsaved and spiritually dead. God doesn't leave us that way.

Paul went on to write, "But you are not in the flesh but in the spirit if indeed the spirit of God dwells in you" (see Romans 8:9 NASB). To be in the Spirit is to be born again, to become a new creature in Christ through the in-dwelling presence of the Holy Spirit. Notice that anyone who does not have the spirit of Christ does not belong to Him. Therefore, to be in the Spirit is to have experienced godly sorrow that leads to repentance, a repentance that leads to salvation. It is to repent and believe the gospel.

To walk in the Spirit is to be controlled by the Spirit of God who lives in us. Now control doesn't mean we walk around like zombies or robots, waiting for heaven to move some levers so we can function. It is to be consistently under the influence of the Holy Spirit who now resides on the inside of every believer to lead, guide, and conform us to the image of Christ. Therefore, every believer is in the Spirit because the Spirit of Christ lives in us and we will never be outside of Christ again. In Him we live, in Him we move, and in Jesus we have our being.

Now that we are in the Spirit, we can worship God in the Spirit and live under the truth and freedom of the New Covenant. Under the Old Covenant, its adherents were spiritually dead, worshipping God under the law and controlled by the sinful nature. Therefore, God could not take up residence in them because of their sin. The sacrifices of the law covered their sin, but it did not cleanse or eliminate it. Because of the death of Christ on the cross, we are free from the condemnation of the Law and the control of the sinful nature, escaping the wrath of God. We are able to be the dwelling place of God in which the face of God can be seen in and through us, His body and bride and the Church, giving hope and being a light to the elect who have yet to be saved.

When you are led by the Spirit, you will have a life of joy and righteousness, but there will be opposition from the enemy of our souls who does not want us to come into these benefits. He hates God and, consequently, hates His people, always trying to hinder or steal the benefits that come by being Spirit led. That is the reason why so many fall short of their full blessing in Christ because they don't know how to resist the devil, not even aware at times they are wrestling with him and not people or circumstances (see 2 Corinthians 10:1-3). One area the enemy seems to attack especially in new believers is their confident knowledge that they are indeed saved. Let's look at how you can know and be assured of what the Lord has done for you in the next chapter.

CHAPTER
11

THE PROOF AND ASSURANCE OF SALVATION

What is the proof and assurance of our salvation? In other words, what is the evidence and the confidence we are truly born again and know we are saved? To answer that, we will look to the Apostle John who wrote the Gospel of John, First, Second and Third John, and the book of Revelation.

This chapter will bring all the pieces together to show us the operation and role of the Kingdom of God in the life of the believer. God did not save us to leave us in the same fallen condition in which He found us. There is something wrong when a person who made a public profession and confession of Christ by praying the sinner's prayer continues living the same way. That is inconsistent with what the Bible teaches.

The problem we are seeing in our day is that we have people who are confessing to be saved while they are living a lifestyle totally inconsistent with what the Bible teaches. We also have a belief system that says if we hold them accountable and point this out, we are judging them and violating the teaching of Christ that we are not to judge. This passage of Scripture is probably one of the few that most so-called Christians can quote: "Judge not lest yea be judged" (Matthew 7:1 KJV). In that verse, Jesus was talking about unjustly judging a person based on our own standard of judgment while we are engaged in the same activity.

He was not warning us to avoid judging but rather to judge based on the biblical standard, as long as we are complying with that ourselves, not by our own ability but by the power of the Holy Spirit living in us. Therefore, we are not looking down at someone to condemn them but extending a hand to help them rise up by the power of the Holy Spirit to comply with what the Bible teaches. This is only possible through the ability of the Holy Spirit within the true believer's heart.

The Apostle Paul does not teach us to condone sinful activity in the church but rather to hold one another accountable to the teachings of God's word. In fact, he tells the Corinthian church that they are not to fellowship with those who call themselves believers yet are living a lifestyle in opposition to what he and the other apostles had taught them from the Scriptures:

> I wrote to you in my epistle not to keep company with sexually immoral people. Yet I certainly did not mean with the sexually immoral people of this world, or with the covetous, or extortioners, or idolaters, since then you would need to go out of the world. But now I have written to you not to keep company with anyone named a brother, who is sexually immoral, or covetous, or an idolater, or a reviler, or a drunkard, or an extortioner—not even to eat with such a person. For what have I

to do with judging those also who are outside? Do you not judge those who are inside? But those who are outside God judges. Therefore "put away from yourselves the evil person" (1 Corinthians 5:9-13).

We see that the Bible does not teach that we are not to judge or hold believers accountable to the standards of God's word. If they are unrepentant and unwilling to comply with the word of God, Paul instructed us not to even eat or fellowship with them but apply Christian disciplinary action, which could include excommunication.

Having said that, I want to point out the Bible teaches there are two things that must precede biblical salvation: godly sorrow and repentance. In fact, the Bible says godly sorrow leads to repentance and repentance to a salvation not to be repented of (see 2 Corinthians 7:10). We must experience godly sorrow for our sins for which the consequence is eternal damnation. Godly sorrow should lead us to want to repent and believe the gospel that leads to salvation. Jesus said on more than one occasion that we need to repent and believe the gospel.

Having repented of our sins and put our faith in the finished work of Christ on the cross, there must be some evidence or assurance of the fact that we are now truly born again and new creatures in Christ. John the Apostle wrote three epistles specifically written so the individual believer would have an assurance of salvation.

First John 5:13 tells us why the letter was written: "These things I have written to you who believe in the name of the Son of God, that you may know that you have eternal life, and that you may continue to believe in the name of the Son of God." Notice he wrote this letter to the ones who believe in the name of Jesus. He was not writing to nonbelievers but rather to those who have put their faith in Jesus and His finished work on the cross. The Bible also tells us that "this is eternal life, that they may know You, the only true God, and Jesus Christ whom You have sent" (John 17:3).

Salvation brings us into a relationship with God the Father through His Son's death on the cross. His resurrection delivers salvation to us through the indwelling presence of His Spirit in our hearts that saves, sustains, and empowers us to live for and serve the one and only triune God. Anyone who has the Son has life; anyone who has not the Son does not have life. What kind of life? This life is called eternal life, the very life of Christ! "The thief does not come except to steal, and to kill, and to destroy. I have come that they may have life, and that they may have it more abundantly" (John 10:10).

Jesus by the Spirit imparts to us His abundant life (eternal life) and everything that goes with it. That still begs the question: How do believers truly know that they have received this life? Well, we don't know if all we have done is pray the sinner's prayer. Please understand, I am not opposed to people praying the sinner's prayer because I have used and will continue to use it in helping a person accept Christ. Just reciting that prayer, however, will not ensure salvation, even if someone is sincere.

People get saved by actually doing what the sinner's prayer says, which is to truly experience godly sorrow that moves them emotionally and practically to repentance. They must understand that their only hope of salvation is in Christ and in Christ alone. For these things to occur, there must be a clear presentation of the gospel to them. Thus, we see salvation goes far beyond just reciting a prayer. There must be the engaging of the mind, emotions, and the will. The elements of saving faith are:

- Mental: their minds must understand the gospel and the truth about Christ and their sinful condition.

- Emotional: having embraced the truthfulness of those facts, they should be moved to godly sorrow for their sin and rejoice over God's mercy and grace.

- Volitional: the act or power of using one's will. They must freely submit their will to Christ and trust in Him as their only hope of salvation.

The reason John had to clarify why he was writing this letter (so believers would know they had eternal life) was because there were false teachers and prophets in the church who were teaching strange things about God, Jesus, and sin, confusing and leading some believers into error. His intention was to set the record straight while restoring the confidence of the believers and exposing the false teaching and teachers.

These doctrines distorting and corrupting the fundamental teachings of the apostles were the beginning of what came to be known as Gnosticism. These strange teachings became an even greater threat to the church than the argument of law and grace being preached by the Judaizers. These Judaizers were Christians teaching it was necessary to adopt Jewish customs and practices, especially those found in the law of Moses (like physical circumcision) if the Gentiles hoped to be saved.

Gnosticism comes from the Greek word *gnosis* meaning knowledge. This knowledge, however, was not a knowledge that could be obtained through studying books or observation. It was a mystical, supernatural wisdom that only certain people could obtain. It came in a variety of forms that evolved through the years. Many describe it as a religious philosophy that was in the world before the Church began. This philosophy began to be adapted and mixed into the religious teachings of the Church through Greek philosophers.

The Gnostics believed that the visible, physical world was inherently and altogether evil—only spirit was good. This philosophy was beginning to pervert the teaching of the Church by leading to misconceptions about the nature of Christ. Since anything physical is evil, the Gnostics taught that Christ could not have come in the flesh. He only seemed to be flesh and was really a phantom or ghost-like apparition. This is why John in his letter hammered home the point that Christ was physically here in the flesh—and John knew it to be true because he had handled and touched Him—and that He was physically raised from the dead because John witnessed Him. First John 1:1-4 states,

> That which was from the beginning, which we have heard, which we have seen with our eyes, which we have looked upon, and our hands have handled, concerning the Word of life—the life was manifested, and we have seen, and bear witness, and declare to you that eternal life which was with the Father and was manifested to us—that which we have seen and heard we declare to you, that you also may have fellowship with us; and truly our fellowship is with the Father and with His Son Jesus Christ. And these things we write to you that your joy may be full.

And First John 4:2-3 says,

> By this you know the Spirit of God: Every spirit that confesses that Jesus Christ has come in the flesh is of God, and every spirit that does not confess that Jesus Christ has come in the flesh is not of God. And this is the spirit of the Antichrist, which you have heard was coming, and is now already in the world.

Notice John continued to emphasize that Jesus came in the flesh. This was important because if what the Gnostics taught was true and Jesus did not come in the flesh, then it became impossible for Christ to die for the sins of humanity. There can be no true Christian atonement to liberate believers from sin and the wrath of God if Jesus did not exist in the flesh.

Second John 7 reads, "For many deceivers have gone out into the world who do not confess Jesus Christ as coming in the flesh. This is a deceiver and an antichrist." Again, John points out that Jesus Christ came in a real and physical body.

He wanted his readers to know that Jesus was truly God in the flesh and was not an apparition or a ghost–like being.

Gnostics also affected some through their teaching that the body was evil and should on one hand be punished or abused and on the other hand taught that, since the spirit and the body were two entirely different entities, then each should be able to take their different paths, because neither could affect the other. Therefore, one could engage in all types of immorality because it didn't matter—the flesh was irrelevant and had no bearing on spiritual things. Therefore, they could completely deny sin even existed and also completely disregard God's laws. John also pointed out sin was real by writing,

> If we say that we have no sin, we deceive ourselves, and the truth is not in us. If we confess our sins, He is faithful and just to forgive us *our* sins and to cleanse us from all unrighteousness. If we say that we have not sinned, we make Him a liar, and His word is not in us.

John emphasized the need for obedience to God's laws and equated the true love of God with obedience to His commandments. The Gnostics maintained that since there was no written revelation about God, the average person could not know Him without some special revelation not revealed to everyone. The Gnostic version of God was one who was very much in the dark—unknowable and shrouded in mystery and darkness. John had to write his letters to deal with all the false teaching the Gnostic teachers had spread through the Church. Because of this, he gave readers a way to know that they were truly born again with an assurance that they have eternal life. First John 1:5-10 says,

> This is the message which we have heard from Him and declare to you, that God is light and in Him is no darkness at all. If we say that we have fellowship with Him, and walk in darkness, we lie and do not practice the truth. But if we walk in

the light as He is in the light, we have fellowship with one another, and the blood of Jesus Christ His Son cleanses us from all sin. If we say that we have no sin, we deceive ourselves, and the truth is not in us. If we confess our sins, He is faithful and just to forgive us *our* sins and to cleanse us from all unrighteousness. If we say that we have not sinned, we make Him a liar, and His word is not in us.

If we read these verses carefully, we learn that being in fellowship with God and salvation are synonymous terms. John was not talking about two Christians: one in fellowship with God and one out of fellowship with God. He was not saying that salvation brought us into fellowship with God but when we sin it takes us out of fellowship with God, while still being saved but unable to fellowship or commune with God.

What he was saying was that because we are in fellowship with God, we are saved. Because we are saved, we are in fellowship with God—those statements mean the same thing. When we are truly saved or in fellowship with God, the blood of Jesus Christ His Son cleanses us from all sin. This is true because we have been justified and declared righteous, freed from the guilt and the penalty of sin. It also includes the imputation of the righteousness of Christ to our spiritual account, which causes us to always be acceptable to God.

Think of this imputed righteousness, which we discussed in Chapter 6, as a robe of righteousness that covers all the areas of life that have not yet been conformed to the image of Christ. God works under that robe of righteousness to *impart* His righteousness, conforming us little by little to the image of Christ and thus making us holy. The robe allows God to continue working on and in us while He is conforming us, until we look and act like Him. Then one day in eternity, He will pull off the robe and behold an image that is as if He is looking into a mirror and seeing the image Christ.

John was not saying that there are two types of

Christians—one in fellowship with God and one out of fellowship with God. He was teaching that all true Christians are saved and in fellowship with God. The true believer sins but cannot continue in sin as a lifestyle. When we are truly saved, we become partners, heirs, and joint heirs with Christ. We are participants with God, we communicate with God, and all that He has is given to us. No Christians can remain in sin as a lifestyle because the internal presence of the Spirit of God will convict them until they repent and confess their sin to God.

He that is born of God cannot sin means we cannot practice sin as a lifestyle because we have a new nature, the divine nature of God, that will not allow us to do so. There will be evidence of salvation through a continuous conforming of us to the image of Christ. He who began a good work in us is able to complete it (see Philippians 1:6). It is God that works in a man both to will and to do his good pleasure (see Philippians 2:13). Earlier we looked at First John 1:5-6, which states,

> This is the message which we have heard from Him and declare to you, that God is light and in Him is no darkness at all. If we say that we have fellowship with Him, and walk in darkness, we lie and do not practice the truth. But if we walk in the light as He is in the light, we have fellowship with one another, and the blood of Jesus Christ His Son cleanses us from all sin.

Light here is not just talking about the holiness of God, emphasizing that there is no sin in Him. It teaches that God has revealed to us who He is and what His will is through the Scriptures and through his Son. He is not hiding His identity or His will, but He is making Himself known. This is the opposite of what the false teachers taught through their false teaching, namely that we could not really know Him or what His will is—and that sins of the flesh didn't matter to God.

Therefore, the evidence or test that you are a true Christian is that a true Christian will walk in the light, which is the revelation of who God is and what His will is as taught to us through the Scriptures and His Son. John's point was that if we say we are Christians but walk or live in a way that consistently contradicts what God has revealed about Himself and what He has revealed about His will, we lie. A true Christian will walk in a way that conforms to or complies with the character God that He revealed concerning Himself.

The word *walk* means your behavior in every area of life must conform to what God has said to you about Himself and His will in the Scriptures. *Walk* refers to a habitual, continuous, and consistent lifestyle and not behavior in a moment in time. The Greek word actually means *to walk around* or *to keep on walking*. The true Christian continues to walk in a consistent manner, exhibiting a lifestyle that conforms or complies with the revealed truth of God's word.

John was not talking about sinless perfection because John had already established the fact that Christians sin and miss the mark. He also taught that if people look at the life of a Christian, they will see a person whose whole style of life over a period of time will be one of seeking to conform to God's will. There will be highs and lows, victories and defeats, but a continuous moving forward. You will never see a Christian habitually, continuously, consistently walking in a lifestyle of sin that does not conform to the character of God that is revealed in Scripture.

John was not talking about an act of sin in a moment of time. It is not an accurate picture that God is someone who is following you, waiting for you to do something wrong so He can punish you. A person depicts God as someone who takes a picture when you fail and uses that one instance as evidence that you are not a Christian. That is not an accurate indicator or representation of a person's life or of who God is or how He relates to us. To get an accurate picture would require following that person around with a video camera, recording their lifestyle for a year. Only then could someone get an accurate picture of that person's life and walk with the Lord. Then we could see if they are seeking to walk in a way that conforms to what God says about Himself and His will.

A true Christian will manifest some areas of imperfection and failure while still striving to be like God. We will see that when he or she sins, there will be brokenness, sorrow, shame, and internal conviction that will cause them to cry out to God, confess their sin, and plead for forgiveness. When they receive those things from God, they move forward, not in their own strength or power, but by the power of the indwelling presence of the Holy Spirit.

What I have described is the true test of assurance of salvation that you walk in the light as He is the light. This is what seeking the kingdom of God is all about: God revealing to us areas of our lives that are not like or in alignment with His will. When He does, we seek and cry out to God to conquer those areas and comply with His work to conform us to the image of Christ through the power of the Holy Spirit. In the next chapter, let me summarize for you everything we have discussed as we close out our look at *The Born Again Panacea Syndrome*.

CHAPTER
12

SUMMARY
CHAPTER

In summary, I defined the Born Again Panacea Syndrome as the belief that the born again experience in and of itself is the cure for everything wrong in life. In reality, it is the key that unlocks the door, removes the blinders, and permits us to see the real answer to all of life's problems, which is the kingdom of God. The Kingdom is the rule, reign, dominion, and governmental control of God in the heart of a person.

This is the reason Jesus instructed His disciples to make their primary priority to seek the kingdom of God. Please understand, I am not saying that the born again experience is elementary, but rather the door one must go through to receive the abundance of what God has to offer to those who belong to Him. It is the cornerstone that everything must rest upon; without it there is no hope of eternal victory!

We began by identifying in detail the human condition in Chapter One, including the cause of the Fall of humanity. In chapter 2, we begin our journey with God through the born again experience, explaining its importance. In chapter 3, we defined and explained the concept of the kingdom of God and discussed what the keys of the kingdom are that Jesus revealed and gave to Peter. In chapters 4 and 5, we took an in depth look at the importance of water baptism and the baptism of the Holy Spirit.

In chapter 6, we continued our journey with God by coming to a biblical understanding of what it means to be a friend of God. We saw all the wonderful benefits that are afforded to those who earn the privilege of being called the friend of God and what that friendship actually means.

In chapter 7 we looked at some typology as it relates to the law of the Nazirite and our salvation. Chapter 8 dealt with the mistakes and failures we have made in our past, and how the enemy attempts to use these ghosts of our past to keep us from moving forward and prevent us from being conformed to the image of Christ. It also discussed the importance of renewing our minds.

Chapter 9 is where we gave full instructions on beginning the process of being conformed to the image of Christ by the renewing of our minds, further proving the point that being born again alone will not take us where we want to be. Instead, we must fully understand the concept of the kingdom of God and begin to seek to come under his Lordship.

Chapter 10 gave us a clear understanding of what it actually means to be in the Spirit. This chapter helped us understand what it means to worship God in spirit and in truth. And that brought us to chapter 12, "The Proof and Assurance Of Our Salvation." This should have left no doubt that it is possible to know whether or not you are a true Christian.

People suffering from the Born Again Panacea syndrome sees no need in doing anything but to simply be happy they are saved and on their way to heaven. They are not motivated to fast, pray, renew their minds, or do the things that will help them be conformed to the image of Christ. They expect God to do it all without any participation of their own in the process. The only way to combat and cure this Syndrome is by being established in a good church with mature leaders who teach sound doctrine. In other words, people must be discipled—it will not float down from heaven automatically.

If you find yourself suffering from this Syndrome, find a good church home with sound teachers and learn all you can, for God has more for you than simply waiting to go to heaven someday. He wants to bring heaven down now, but only for those who have accepted His terms of repentance, water baptism, baptism of the Holy Spirit, and a life of picking up their cross and following Jesus.

AFTERWORD

After reading this book on the human condition and the importance of being born again, perhaps your eyes have been opened to the fact that you are not a Christian. If you have no true assurance that you are saved, I would be remiss if I did not extend an opportunity to turn your life over to Christ. Please allow me to introduce to you the Lover and Redeemer of your soul, Jesus Christ. If the Holy Spirit is dealing with you, there will be great sorrow for your sinful condition, a desire to repent, and a genuine fear of your eternal destination. If these exist and you have a desire to give your life to Christ, please pray this prayer with me. Before you pray, please understand this prayer will not save you, but godly sorrow, repentance, and faith in the death, burial, and the resurrection of Christ will.

Dear Jesus,

I realize that I am a sinner, but it is not my desire to continue in the lifestyle that I am living. Nor is it my desire to experience eternal damnation and separation from you. I repent of my sin and ask you to forgive me and to come into my heart and be my Savior. Your Word says that godly sorrow leads to repentance and repentance to a salvation. I ask you, Father, that You would grant me the faith to embrace the gospel of Jesus' death, burial, and resurrection.

Your Word says that if I confess with my mouth the Lord Jesus and believe in my heart that You have raised Him from the dead, I would be saved. Your Word also says that with the heart, people believe unto righteousness and with the mouth confession is made to salvation. I confess with my mouth the Lord Jesus and believe in my heart that You have raised Him from the dead. You promised that whoever calls on the name of the Lord will be saved. Lord Jesus, I thank You for saving me and becoming my Savior.

If you have truly given your life to Christ, please follow the instructions of this book and find a good church to attend where you can also be baptized in water and the Holy Spirit.

I would love to hear from you.
My email address is louisotey1@verizon.net
or you can contact me on Facebook.